China, Internet Freedom, and U.S. Policy

Thomas Lum, Coordinator
Acting Section Research Manager/Specialist in Asian Affairs

Patricia Moloney Figliola
Specialist in Internet and Telecommunications Policy

Matthew C. Weed
Analyst in Foreign Policy Legislation

July 13, 2012

Congressional Research Service

7-5700

www.crs.gov

R42601

CRS Report for Congress
Prepared for Members and Committees of Congress

Summary

The People's Republic of China (PRC) has the world's largest number of Internet users, estimated at 500 million people. Despite government efforts to limit the flow of online news, Chinese Internet users are able to access unprecedented amounts of information, and political activists have utilized the Web as a vital communications tool. In recent years, Twitter-like microblogging has surged, resulting in dramatic cases of dissident communication and public comment on sensitive political issues. However, the Web has proven to be less of a democratic catalyst in China than many observers had hoped. The PRC government has one of the most rigorous Internet censorship systems, which relies heavily upon cooperation between the government and private Internet companies. Some U.S. policy makers have been especially critical of the compliance of some U.S. Internet communications and technology (ICT) companies with China's censorship and policing activities.

The development of the Internet and its use in China have raised U.S. congressional concerns, including those related to human rights, trade and investment, and cybersecurity. The link between the Internet and human rights, a pillar of U.S. foreign policy towards China, is the main focus of this report. Congressional interest in the Internet in China is tied to human rights concerns in a number of ways. These include the following:

- The use of the Internet as a U.S. policy tool for promoting freedom of expression and other rights in China,

- The use of the Internet by political dissidents in the PRC, and the political repression that such use often provokes,

- The role of U.S. Internet companies in both spreading freedom in China and complying with PRC censorship and social control efforts, and

- The development of U.S. Internet freedom policies globally.

Since 2006, congressional committees and commissions have held nine hearings on Internet freedom and related issues, with a large emphasis on China. In response to criticism, in 2008, Yahoo!, Microsoft, Google, and other parties founded the Global Network Initiative, a set of guidelines that promotes awareness, due diligence, and transparency regarding the activities of ICT companies and their impacts on human rights, particularly in countries where governments frequently violate the rights of Internet users to freedom of expression and privacy. In the 112th Congress, the Global Online Freedom Act (H.R. 3605) would require U.S. companies to disclose any censorship or surveillance technology that they provide to Internet-restricting countries. It also would bar U.S. companies from selling technology that could be used for the purposes of censorship or surveillance in such countries.

For over a decade, the United States government has sought to promote global Internet freedom, particularly in China and Iran. In 2006, the Bush Administration established the Global Internet Freedom Task Force, which was renamed the NetFreedom Task Force under the Obama Administration. Congress provided $95 million for global Internet freedom programs between 2008 and 2012. The Broadcasting Board of Governors has spent approximately $2 million annually during the past decade to help enable Internet users in China and other Internet-restricting countries to access its websites, such as Voice of America and Radio Free Asia.

Some experts argue that support for counter-censorship technology, which has long dominated the U.S. effort to promote global Internet freedom, has had an important but limited impact. Obstacles to Internet freedom in China and elsewhere include not only censorship but also the following: advances in government capabilities to monitor and attack online dissident activity; tight restrictions on social networking; and the lack of popular pressure for greater Internet freedom. As part of a broadening policy approach, the U.S. government has sponsored a widening range of Internet freedom programs, including censorship circumvention technology; privacy protection and online security; training civil society groups in effective uses of the Web for communications, organizational, and advocacy purposes; and spreading awareness of Internet freedom.

Contents

Appendixes

Contacts

Policy Overview[1]

The People's Republic of China (PRC) has the world's largest number of Internet users, estimated at 500 million people, including an estimated 300 million people with accounts on Twitter-like micro blogging sites. Despite government efforts to limit the flow of information, Chinese Internet users are able to access unprecedented amounts of information, and the Web has served as a lifeline for political dissidents, social activists, and civil society actors. "Netizens" have helped to curb some abuses of government authority and compelled some officials to conduct affairs more openly.[2] The Web also has enabled the public to engage in civil discourse on a national level. Some government departments have begun to solicit online public input on policy issues. However, the Internet has proven to be less of a catalyst for democratic change in China than many foreign observers had initially expected or hoped. Along with its extensive internal security apparatus, China also has an aggressive and multi-faceted Internet censorship system. In 2011, *Freedom House* ranked China as one of the five countries with the lowest levels of Internet and "new media" freedom. According to some estimates, roughly 70 Chinese citizens are serving prison sentences for writing about politically sensitive topics online.[3]

The development of the Internet and its use in China have raised U.S. congressional concerns, including those related to human rights, trade and investment, and cybersecurity. Congressional interest in the Internet in China is linked to human rights in a number of ways. These include the use of the Internet as a U.S. policy tool for promoting freedom of expression and other rights in China; the use of the Internet by political dissidents in the PRC and the political repression that such use often provokes; and the role of U.S. Internet companies in both spreading freedom in China and cooperating with PRC censorship and social control efforts.

In addition to the effectiveness of censorship, some studies show that the vast majority of Internet users in China do not engage the medium for political purposes. Although a small community of dissidents and activists use the Web to broach political topics, they reportedly make up a small minority—less than 10% of all users according to some estimates. Between 1% and 8% of Web users in China use proxy servers and virtual private networks to get around government-erected Internet firewalls to access censored content—both political and non-political.[4]

The widespread satisfaction reportedly felt by many Chinese Internet users has reduced public pressure for greater freedom. Although netizens have frequently protested against government actions aimed at further controlling Web content and use, the Internet in China offers a wide and attractive range of services, making restrictions almost unnoticeable to many users. Furthermore, some experts argue that the Internet in China has created an illusion of democracy by allowing

---

[1] Written by Thomas Lum, Specialist in Asian Affairs.

[2] Yanqi Tong and Shaohua Lei, "Creating Public Opinion Pressure in China: Large-Scale Internet Protest," *East Asian Institute (Singapore) Background Brief No. 534*, June 17, 2010.

[3] U.S. Department of State, 2011 *Human Rights Report: China*, May 2012; Reporters Without Borders, http://en rsf.org/report-china,57 html; *Freedom on the Net* 2011, http://www.freedomhouse.org/report/freedom-net/freedom-net-2011. The top countries, in order of restrictions, are: Iran, Burma, Cuba, China, Tunisia, Vietnam, and Saudi Arabia.

[4] Ed Zhang,"Does Blogs' Blooming Mean Schools of Thought Can Contend?" *South China Morning Post*, December 4, 2011; Rebecca MacKinnon, "Bloggers and Censors: Chinese Media in the Internet Age," *China Studies Center*, May 18, 2007; John Pomfret, "U.S. Risks Ire with Decision to Fund Software Maker Tied to Falun Gong," *Washington Post*, May 12, 2010; Rebecca MacKinnon, *Consent of the Networked*, Basic Books: New York, 2012.

people to vent their opinions online and by providing venues for debate on some political and policy issues.[5] Moreover, many Chinese accept the government's justification that it regulates the Internet in order to control illegal, harmful, or dangerous online content, services, and activities, such as pornography, gambling, slander, cyberattacks, and social networking by criminal organizations.

U.S. efforts to promote Internet freedom have broadened. Since the early 2000s, policy makers have focused on supporting censorship circumvention techniques and their use in China, protecting the privacy of Chinese Internet users, and discouraging or preventing U.S. information and communications technology companies from aiding Beijing's censorship efforts and public surveillance system. According to some analysts, counter-censorship technology has proven to have a vital, but limited, impact on the promotion of freedom and democracy in the PRC. They have advocated a broader approach or the development of a more comprehensive and robust mix of tools and education for "cyber dissidents" and online activists in China and elsewhere, including the following: software and training to help dissidents and civil society actors communicate securely through evading surveillance, detecting spyware, and guarding against cyberattacks; archiving and disseminating information that censors have removed from the Internet; developing means of maintaining Internet access when the government has shut it down entirely; and providing training in online communication, organization, and advocacy.[6]

Internet Censorship

The PRC government employs a variety of methods to control online content and expression, including website or IP address blocking and keyword filtering by routers at the country's eight Internet "gateways,"[7] telecommunications company data centers, and Internet portals; regulating and monitoring Internet service providers, Internet cafes, and university bulletin board systems; registering websites and blogs; and occasional arrests of high-profile "cyber dissidents" or crackdowns on Internet service providers. Some analysts argue that even though the PRC government cannot control all Internet content and use, its selective targeting creates an undercurrent of fear and promotes self-censorship. Blocked websites, social networking sites, and file sharing sites include Radio Free Asia, Voice of America (Chinese language), international human rights websites, many Taiwanese news sites, Facebook, Twitter, and YouTube. Online English language news sites, including the Voice of America, the *New York Times*, and the *Washington Post*, are generally accessible or only occasionally or selectively censored. Commonly barred Internet searches and micro-blog postings include those with direct and indirect or disguised references to Tibet, the Tiananmen suppression of 1989, Falun Gong, PRC leaders and dissidents who have been involved in recent, politically sensitive events, democracy,

---

[5] Rebecca MacKinnon, "Is Web 2.0 a Wash for Free Speech in China?" *RConversation*, http://rconversation.blogs.com; MacKinnon, *Consent of the Networked*, op. cit.

[6] Rebecca MacKinnon, "Global Internet Freedom and the U.S. Government," *RConversation*, March 15, 2010, http://rconversation.blogs.com/rconversation/2010/03/global-internet-freedom-and-the-us-government html; Ethan Zuckerman, "Internet Freedom: Beyond Circumvention," *My Heart's in Accra*, February 22, 2010, http://facthai.wordpress.com/2010/03/02/internet-freedom-beyond-circumvention-ethan-zuckerman/; Kelley Currie, "Winning the Battle over Internet Freedom," *CBS News*, October 27, 2010; Rebecca MacKinnon, Testimony before the House Committee on Foreign Affairs, Subcommittee on Africa, Global Health, and Human Rights, December 8, 2011.

[7] Routers at these gateways and Internet service providers, using algorithms as well as human editors, block websites and politically sensitive keywords.

---

highly charged foreign affairs issues, and sexual material. The government reportedly also has hired thousands of students to express pro-government views on websites, bulletin boards, and chat rooms.

The Public-Private Nexus

Some experts argue that China's success in maintaining control over the Internet is based largely upon its reliance on private sector actors and profit motives. By imposing non-coercive incentives for compliance, the government has been able to maintain a fairly reliable system of control at relatively little cost. In order to maintain their business licenses and operate in China, domestic and foreign Internet companies are required to abide by a rough set of guidelines issued by central and local government agencies—and thus encouraged to practice self-censorship. Companies that have learned how to prosper in this environment include Baidu, China's largest search engine, Sina Weibo, which offers a Twitter-like micro-blogging platform, and Tencent, which provides instant messaging services.

Large Internet portals are estimated to each employ hundreds of people to filter online discussion.[8] Sina Weibo is said to employ approximately 1,000 people to monitor and censor expression on its social networking service.[9] In May 2012, Sina instituted a point system in which customers are given a number of starting points that are deducted if the they post "harmful" content. If a customer's cache of points falls to zero, then his or her account is terminated.[10] Service providers are often torn between providing interesting content and allowing wide-ranging discussion, on the one hand, and complying with government guidelines, on the other, both of which can affect their economic survival.

Another aspect of the PRC government's ability to control online information is the degree to which the experience of the Internet user in China resembles that of Internet users in freer environments elsewhere. The abundant array of offerings on China's Internet, vibrant news coverage, public discourse on a range of issues, and selective rather than widespread use of coercive measures, such as arrests of netizens who use the Internet for political purposes, has diluted opposition to China's censorship regime. Although their foreign counterparts are blocked, Chinese can search terms on Baidu, engage in social networking on RenRen and Kaixinwang, and blog or "Tweet" via Sohu and Sina platforms. These phenomena have even been referred to by Chinese officials as "Internet democracy." One U.S. expert states that "China's 500 million Internet users feel free and are less fearful of their government than in the past. The communications revolution has transformed China in many ways, but the Communist Party has thus far succeeded—against all odds and expectations—in controlling it to remain in power."[11]

---

[8] MacKinnon, *Consent of the Networked*, op. cit.

[9] Loretta Chao and Josh Chin, "China Eases Crackdown on Internet," *Wall Street Journal*, April 2, 2012; Rebecca MacKinnon, Testimony before the House Committee on Foreign Affairs, Subcommittee on Africa, Global Health, and Human Rights, December 8, 2011.

[10] Sina's management said the aim of the measures is not to impose greater censorship but rather to create order. Offenses include spreading rumors, engaging in personal attacks, calling for protests, and using homonyms to disguise comments on censored topics. Loretta Chao and Josh Chin, "China Microblog Site Regulates Talk—Users of Service Are Punished for Posting Content That Is Deemed Harmful," *Wall Street Journal*, May 30, 2012; Michael Wines, "Crackdown on Chinese Bloggers Who Fight the Censors with Puns," *New York Times*, May 28, 2012.

[11] MacKinnon, *Consent of the Networked*, op. cit.

Censorship Circumvention

Since Internet-use became widespread in China in the mid-2000s, the government and netizens have engaged in a game of cat and mouse, with new communications platforms challenging the government's efforts to control the Web, followed by crackdowns or new regulations, and then a repeat of the cycle. Bulletin and message boards, personal Web sites, blogs, micro blogs, and other communication outlets have allowed for an unprecedented amount of information and public comment on social and other issues. Although the state has the capability to block the dissemination of news or shut down the Internet, as it did in Xinjiang for several months following the social unrest that erupted there in July 2009, it often cannot do so before such events are publicized, if only fleetingly, online.

For Chinese Internet users in search of blocked information from outside the PRC's Internet gateways, or "great firewall," circumventing government controls (also known as *fanqiang* or "scaling the wall") is made possible by downloading special software. These methods mainly include proxy servers, which are free but somewhat cumbersome, and virtual private networks (VPNs), which are available at a small cost (roughly $40.00) but also enable secure communication.[12] Proxy servers and VPNs enable some motivated Internet users to avoid censorship, but impose just enough inconvenience to keep foreign information out of the reach of most Chinese users. The use of these tools is tolerated by the government as long as it remains politically manageable, according to some observers. However, the government occasionally has attempted to curtail their use, as in 2011, when users of VPNs began to experience interference with their access to foreign Web sites.[13]

While remaining vigilant against Internet activities that it perceives may give rise to organized or potentially destabilizing political activities, the PRC government has been careful not to unnecessarily provoke the ire of the general online population. Nor does it want to alienate China's international business community, which relies upon Internet services as well as VPNs. In one dramatic example, the government backed down when confronted by an outpouring of domestic and foreign opposition to an initiative designed to filter content. In 2009, the Ministry of Information and Information Technology issued a directive requiring the installation of special software ("Green Dam Youth Escort" software), ostensibly created to block harmful content potentially affecting children, on all Chinese computers sold after July 1, 2009, including those imported from abroad. Many Chinese Internet users and international human rights activists, foreign governments, chambers of commerce, and computer manufacturers openly opposed the policy, arguing that the software would undermine computer operability, that it could be used to expand censorship to include political content, and that it may incorporate pirated software and weaken Internet security.[14] On June 30, 2009, the PRC government announced that mandatory installation of the software would be delayed for an indefinite period and that any future policy would involve public input.[15] One clear exception to this method of selective targeting, however,

---

[12] Amy Nip, "HK Firms Help Mainlanders Get around the 'Great Firewall'," *South China Morning Post*, March 15, 2011.

[13] MacKinnon, *Consent of the Networked*, op. cit.; Charles Arthur, "China Cracks Down on VPN Use," *The Guardian*, May 13, 2011.

[14] In January 2010, a U.S. software firm filed a lawsuit against the Chinese government for copyright infringement, unfair competition, and other legal violations in connection with the Green Dam program. Agence France-Presse, "U.S. Software Firm Sues Chinese Government for US$2.2 Billion," *South China Morning Post*, January 6, 2010.

[15] "Green Dam Launch 'Not Handled Well'," http://www.chinaview.cn, August 14, 2009.

is Tibet, where Internet censorship is often indiscriminate and repression of free speech and communication harsher than other parts of China.[16]

Recent Developments

In the past decade, various online communications platforms have repeated a pattern of boom and decline. In such cycles, Chinese Internet users enthusiastically adopted new technologies to express their opinions on current issues. They then faced growing government restrictions, but also new opportunities as circumvention tools developed or new services became available. The first medium that offered this possibility on a mass scale was bulletin boards attached to websites, followed by personal websites, and then blogs. The most recent sensation in China is Twitter-like microblogging.

Weibo (Microblogs)

In the short space of two years, Micro-blog sites (*weibo*), similar to Twitter,[17] have become, according to some experts, the country's "most important public sphere," the "most prominent place for free speech," and the most important source of news.[18] There are reportedly 300 million microbloggers on platforms provided by major Chinese Internet service providers such as Sina and Tencent. They have been at the forefront of exposing official malfeasance, corruption, and other sensitive news. In July 2011, for example, micro bloggers broke the news about the high speed train crash near the city of Wenzhou that killed 40 passengers, as the government attempted to control coverage and official news outlets delayed reporting. Microblogs have become so popular that news sites and online portals have started highlighting "hot microblogs." Chinese government departments, elites, opinion makers, trend setters, and others, including government ministries and officials, police departments, state media outlets, academics, celebrities, and candidates for local people's congresses have opened microblog accounts, as has the U.S. Embassy in Beijing.

Chen Guangcheng's Escape and the Internet

In the case of Chen Guangcheng, the blind legal advocate who in April 2012 escaped extra-judicial house arrest in Shandong province, found refuge in the U.S. Embassy in Beijing, and ultimately was allowed to travel with his family to New York City, both Chinese *weibo* and Twitter helped keep supporters and reporters apprised of his status.[19] The comment sections of some Chinese official news sites reportedly were flooded with expressions of support for Chen and U.S. Ambassador Locke, who was instrumental in helping him. Chinese authorities closed the microblog accounts of some prominent political commentators and banned search terms related to Chen, including the following: his name, initials, and home town; phrases such as "blind man" and "U.S. Embassy;" code words such as "Shawshank Redemption" and "The Great Escape"—two movies about escaped prisoners; and "UA898"—the United Airlines flight from Beijing to Washington.

---

[16] U.S. Department of State, *Country Reports on Human Rights Practices for 2011*, May 2012.

[17] Twitter is blocked in China but still used by many Chinese, particularly netizens with international connections.

[18] Kathrin Hile, "China's Tweeting Cops Blog to Keep Peace," *Financial Times*, December 5, 2011; Keith B. Richburg, "In China, Microblogging Sites become Free-Speech Platform," *Washington Post*, March 27,2011; Ed Zhang, op. cit..

[19] For further information on Chen Guangcheng, see CRS Report R42554, *U.S.-China Diplomacy Over Chinese Legal Advocate Chen Guangcheng*, by Susan V. Lawrence and Thomas Lum.

The PRC government has struggled to minimize the effects of posts and bloggers that undermine its leadership and policies, often clamping down on Internet communications over a politically sensitive event, then relaxing, only to repeat the repeat the cycle as information about another event leaks out online. It has stepped up pressure on Sina and other companies to censor messages or close accounts that "spread rumors" or "jeopardize the national or public interest."[20] The government has become particularly nervous as news and rumors have spread in the blogosphere regarding the scandal involving purged Chongqing Party Secretary and Politburo member Bo Xilai and the arrest of his wife for the murder of a British businessman. In April 2012, Sina reportedly terminated four *weibo* accounts alleged to have spread rumors in connection with Bo Xilai.[21]

New Regulations

The PRC government has displayed an ongoing nervousness about the Internet's influence on Chinese society and politics and has developed an ever-expanding array of controls. However, it has attempted to enact and enforce restrictions on Internet use judiciously and selectively and to largely induce self-censorship and rely on Internet Service Providers rather than to impose penalties directly, in order to avoid provoking a backlash among China's online community. In 2011, the State Council Information Office established two new agencies, the State Internet Information Office and the Internet News Coordination Bureau, to help consolidate the management of Internet content, which is decentralized to a large degree. In recent years, PRC authorities also have attempted to bolster their ability to monitor Internet users. Although this effort ostensibly has focused upon curtailing Internet pornography, the spread of false information, and other illegal or socially disruptive content, it also has had a dampening effect on political discourse. The central government and localities have attempted to require users to provide their real names or official identification numbers or photos when they apply for an Internet account, website, or blog; post online comments; or patronize Internet cafes or other public places.[22] In 2012, new rules requiring users of social media platforms to register with their real names met with opposition from many Chinese Internet users and a low rate of compliance.[23] Some of these policies reportedly have not been well-enforced, due in part to resistance among service providers which fear that they will adversely affect the popularity of their services.

U.S. Internet Companies in China

As U.S. Internet companies entered the Chinese market in the early 2000s, some of them became directly or indirectly involved in PRC government censorship and surveillance efforts, which concerned some Members of Congress. In 2004, Yahoo! was blamed for providing e-mail account holder information to state security authorities which resulted in the arrests of four Chinese Internet users. In the most high-profile case, the Internet service provider was accused of having provided information about the identity of a Chinese journalist and Yahoo! e-mail account holder,

---

[20] Keith B. Richburg, "China Tightens Control of Microblogs," *Washington Post*, October 5, 2011.

[21] Kathrin Hille, "China Finds It Can't Arrest Rumours on Social Media," *Financial Times*, April 25, 2012.

[22] Even with the use of pseudonyms, the government can track down individuals through their IP addresses.

[23] Phil Muncaster, "China's Police Ignore Real Name Rules ... So Far," *The Register*, March 19, 2012. Reports in the official press indicated both support of and opposition to the new requirements for real name registration. "Weibo Launches Real-Name Registration," *Globaltimes.cn*, March 15, 2012.

Shi Tao. Shi reportedly had forwarded information about state policy regarding the 15th anniversary of the June 4, 1989, demonstrations in Tiananmen via his Yahoo! e-mail account to an overseas democracy group.[24] In March 2005, a PRC court sentenced Shi to 10 years in prison for "leaking state secrets." In 2006, Microsoft shut down the MSN Spaces site of Chinese journalist Zhao Jing (a.k.a. Michael Anti) at the request of the PRC government, after Zhao had expressed support on his blog for a boycott of *Beijing News* following the firing of one of its editors. Human rights activists also criticized Microsoft for blocking words such as "democracy" from MSN Spaces.[25]

Other U.S. and western companies are alleged to have provided technology to the PRC government for censorship and surveillance efforts. For example, in the early 2000s, Cisco Systems, Juniper Networks, Nortel of Canada, and Alcatel of France (now Alcatel-Lucent) reportedly were involved in upgrading China's Internet infrastructure, filtering, and surveillance systems. According to some reports, Cisco Systems sold several thousand routers to China, which some analysts argue helped to facilitate the PRC government's censorship of Internet content and monitoring of Internet users. According to other reports, Cisco also sold technology to China's police force that can be used in the collection and use of data regarding personal background and imaging information, Web browsing history, and e-mail.[26] In 2011, human rights groups filed two lawsuits in U.S. district courts against Cisco Systems on behalf of PRC citizens, claiming that the U.S. company helped PRC authorities to censor the Internet and track and apprehend dissidents and members of the outlawed Falun Gong group.[27] In the same year, Cisco, working with a Chinese company, reportedly agreed to provide networking equipment to be used in Chongqing municipality's city-wide video surveillance system.[28]

In response to criticism, some U.S. ICT companies have argued that they must abide by the laws of the countries in which they operate, and that they are not actively cooperating or collaborating with the PRC government or tailoring their products to suit PRC censorship requirements. Cisco's general counsel has made the following arguments: Cisco does not customize its equipment for China; filtering technologies that are intrinsic to the company's products cannot feasibly be eliminated; Cisco has a written code of conduct that aims to prevent the modification of its products in foreign countries in such as way as to undermine human rights; and Cisco complies with all U.S. government regulations or export controls that restrict the sale of high tech products and crime detection equipment.[29]

---

[24] Peter S. Goodman, "Yahoo Says It Gave China Internet Data," *Washington Post*, September 11, 2005.

[25] In August 2005, Yahoo! bought a roughly 40% stake in the *Alibaba* Group, a Chinese e-commerce business, and turned over management of its Chinese search engine to the company. In 2012, Yahoo! sold half of this share back to Alibaba. In 2007, Yahoo! settled with the families of Shi Tao and Wang Xiaoning and established a Yahoo Human Rights Fund and a fellowship at Georgetown University to support research on the Internet and human rights. In 2010, Microsoft joined Chinese Web portal Sina.com to offer an integrated line of services including instant messaging, blogging, and microblogging, and news. In 2011, Microsoft began offering its Bing search tool through Chinese Web giant *Baidu*.

[26] Steven Mufson, "China Turning to Technology to Hold onto Power," *Washington Post*, April 16, 2006; "Cisco's Role in China's Crackdown in Dispute," *San Francisco Chronicle*, March 11, 2012.

[27] Jim Duffy, "Cisco Faces Second Suit over China Actions," *Network World*, June 10, 2011.

[28] James Temple, "How Bay Area Firms' Tools Aid Repressive Governments," *San Francisco Chronicle*, March 11, 2012.

[29] See Anne Broache, "Senators Weigh New Laws over China Online Censorship," news.cnet.com, May 20, 2008; Mark Chandler, Cisco Systems, Testimony before the Subcommittee on Africa, Global Human Rights and International Operations and the Subcommittee on Asia and the Pacific of the Committee on International Relations, February 15, (continued...)

Some U.S. companies add that despite PRC censorship policies, they nonetheless are enlarging the volume of information available in China and other Internet-restricting countries, and can better press for freedom of expression and protection of privacy while located in these countries. They also claim that Chinese and other Asian and European competitors would fill the void in providing Internet services and technology in their absence. Some Chinese experts have suggested that overall, foreign companies have promoted freedom through the Internet in China, although they also have made troubling compromises with the government.[30]

Google: Cyberattacks and Censorship

From the time Google entered the China market in 2006, the search engine giant and the PRC government clashed over censorship and other issues. Google's Chinese search engine, Google.cn, grew to become the second most widely used information-gathering service in China after *Baidu*, a Chinese company, and was the least censored, according to one study.[31] The company limited its services in China—it offered a search engine but neither Chinese versions of Gmail nor its blogging platform, Blogger—and thus avoided some of the compliance and human rights issues that had faced Yahoo! and Microsoft. On the whole, Google attempted to comply with PRC censorship policies while disassociating itself from them. It provided a message stating that a blocked website was made unavailable due to "local laws, regulations, and policies," suggesting to the Chinese user that information existed, but that the government had closed access to that site.

In January 2010, Google threatened to cease filtering its Chinese search engine or to pull out of China. The company asserted that, in December 2009, Chinese hackers had attacked its Gmail service and corporate network as well as the computer systems of many other large U.S. corporations in the PRC.[32] In what has been dubbed by the press as "Operation Aurora," hackers appeared to have targeted the Gmail accounts of Chinese human rights activists; the intellectual property, including "source codes" or programming languages, of Google and other companies; and information on U.S. weapons systems. In a statement, Google's chief legal officer announced that the company would no longer censor results on Google.cn, even if that meant having to shut down the search engine, and potentially its offices in China.[33]

Chinese discussion boards and micro-blog posts indicated that a small majority of the country's online population—and perhaps a large majority of its most educated Internet users—wanted Google to stay in China, some of them supporting the U.S. company's challenge to the PRC government. A significant minority, many of whom reportedly were acting at the government's

(...continued)

2006; Mark Chandler, Cisco Systems, Testimony before the Senate Committee on the Judiciary, Subcommittee on Human Rights and the Law, May 20, 2008.

[30] "Censored in China," *The Cambridge Student Online*, February 21, 2008.

[31] Tom Krazit, "Google's Censorship Struggles Continue in China," *news.cnet.com*, June 16, 2009; Steven Mufson, "China Faces Backlash from 'Netizens' if Google Leaves," *Washington Post*, January 13, 2010.

[32] Estimates of the number of U.S. information technology, finance, defense, and other companies targeted in this attack ranged from 20 to 34.

[33] Google representatives stated that two Gmail accounts appeared to have been accessed but that the content of e-mail communications had not been breached. "Statement from Google: A New Approach to China," *Washington Post*, January 12, 2010. See also "A New Approach to China," *The Official Google Blog*, January 12, 2010, http://googleblog.blogspot.com/2010/01/new-approach-to-china.html.

behest, adopted pro-Beijing stances or interpreted Google's move as profit-oriented.[34] According to some analysts, the company earned an estimated $300 million to $400 million from its China operations at the time, a "tiny fraction" of its $22 billion in sales worldwide.[35] Although Google confirmed in February 2010 that the attacks had come from mainland China, Beijing denied involvement and defended its Internet policies. The Foreign Ministry stated that foreign companies, including Google, "should respect the laws and regulations, respect the public interest of Chinese people and China's culture and customs and shoulder due social responsibilities."[36]

In March 2010, Google re-routed searches in mainland China to its uncensored Hong Kong site—automatically redirecting users from "Google.cn" to "Google.com.hk." Although neither the Hong Kong government nor Google censors the Hong Kong site, the PRC government can still filter search results for Internet users accessing the site from mainland China. Since Google's action allowed it to avoid participating in China's censorship practices, China's State Council Information Office accused the company of having broken a "written promise" to follow PRC Internet laws. Finally, in June 2010, the day before Google's license to do business in China was due to expire, the company submitted a renewal application saying it would create a new Google.cn landing page, where users could access the uncensored Hong Kong search engine by entering search terms or through a link. Some analysts regarded the decision as a compromise—Google's search engine can still be accessed in mainland China (through Hong Kong), but there is no direct link to the Hong Kong site.[37] After having struggled for several years to build market share, Google's portion of China's search-engine market has fallen from 30% in 2009 to 16% in 2012, while Baidu's share has grown from 58% to over 78% during the same period.[38]

The Global Network Initiative[39]

In response to criticism, particularly of their operations in China, a group of U.S. information and communications technology companies, along with civil society organizations, investors, and academic entities, formed the Global Network Initiative (GNI) in 2008. The GNI aims to promote best practices related to the conduct of U.S. companies in countries with poor Internet freedom records.[40] The GNI adopts a self-regulatory approach to promote due diligence and awareness regarding human rights. A set of principles and supporting mechanisms provide guidance to the ICT industry and its stakeholders on how to protect and advance freedom of expression and the

---

[34] Jessica E. Vascellaro and Aaron Back, "Fallout from Cyber Attack Spreads—Google Investigates China Employees; Rift Emerges Between Yahoo! and Alibaba," *Wall Street Journal*, January 19, 2010; Rebecca MacKinnon, "Google Puts Its Foot Down," *RConversation,* http://rconversation.blogs.com/rconversation/china/index.html, January 13, 2010. Susan Shirk, ed. *Changing Media, Changing China*, Oxford: Oxford University Press, 2011.

[35] Miguel Helft, "For Google, A Threat to China with Little Revenue at Stake," *New York Times*, January 15, 2010.

[36] Gillian Wong, "China Denies Involvement in Google Hackings," *Washington Post*, January 25, 2010; "China Says Google 'No Exception to Law'," Embassy of the People's Republic of China in the United States, January 19, 2010.

[37] Dawn Kawamoto, "Google to Stop Hong Kong Re-Direct in Bid to Renew Content License," *AOL Daily Finance*, June 29, 2010, http://www.dailyfinance.com/2010/06/29/google-china/.

[38] "China Search Engine Market Share by Revenue," *China Internet Watch*, April 25, 2012, http://www.chinainternetwatch.com/1444/china-search-engine-market-share-by-revenue-q1-2012/; Mark Lee, "Google Loses China Search-Engine Market Share, Researcher Says," Bloomberg.com, January 18, 2011; David Pierson and David Sarno, "Bing Gets Foothold in China Market," *Lost Angeles Times*, July 6, 2011.

[39] Written by Patricia Maloney Figliola, Specialist in Internet and Telecommunications Policy.

[40] The GNI website is online at http://www.globalnetworkinitiative.org/index.php. The 2011 GNI annual report is available online at http://www.globalnetworkinitiative.org/files/GNI_2011_Annual_Report.pdf.

---

right to privacy when faced with pressures from governments to take actions that infringe upon these rights.[41] Companies undergo third-party assessments of their compliance with GNI principles. Although some human rights groups have criticized the GNI's guidelines for being weak or too broad, the GNI's supporters argue that the initiative sets realistic goals and creates real incentives for companies to uphold free expression and privacy.[42]

(For the GNI's membership, core documents, and implementation process, see the **Appendix**.)

U.S. Government Actions to Promote Global Internet Freedom[43]

U.S. government efforts to promote and protect Internet freedom operate as a part of overall U.S. cyberspace policy and programs. Released in May 2011, the President's International Strategy for Cyberspace outlines strategic and policy priorities for the global digital infrastructure and networked technology. The Strategy sets out a number of goals that include enabling continued innovation for increasing economic activity, increasing individuals' ability to communicate with one another, safeguarding freedom of expression, association, and other freedoms, and enhancing both individual privacy and national and international security. It stresses using diplomacy to build unified action for creating standards in regulating and operating global digital networks, employing national defense actors to oppose and protect against malicious actors in cyberspace, and focusing development resources on increasing and improving developing countries' digital system capacity and access to such systems by their populations. The Strategy sets out seven policy priorities focusing on opening markets, enhancing security, enforcing relevant law, ensuring military response capabilities, promoting Internet governance, developing capacity and security, and promoting Internet freedom.

Some observers have questioned the ability of the U.S. government to effectively promote Internet freedom and meet the other policy goals of the Strategy and U.S. foreign policy and national security goals generally. The United States also has been criticized for employing many of the most sophisticated surveillance and other security-related technologies on the Internet, both domestically and internationally, and many repressive regimes have used restrictive technologies developed by U.S. companies.[44] In addition, Google has recently reported that several democratic countries including the United States have engaged in their own censorship efforts, significantly increasing their requests for websites or online information to be removed from Google search results.[45]

---

[41] http://www.globalnetworkinitiative.org/index.php

[42] Elisa Massimino, Human Rights First, "Judge the Global Network Initiative by How It Judges Companies," March 31, 2011; Douglass MacMillan, "Google, Yahoo Criticized Over Foreign Censorship," *BusinessWeek*, March 13, 2009.

[43] Written by Matthew C. Weed, Analyst in Foreign Policy Legislation.

[44] Rebecca MacKinnon, "Internet Freedom Starts at Home," *Foreign Policy*, April 3, 2012, http://www.foreignpolicy.com/articles/2012/04/03/The_Worlds_No_1_Threat_to_Internet_Freedom.

[45] Jeffrey Bloomer, "Google: 'Alarming' Rise in U.S. Removal Requests," *Slate*, June 18, 2012, http://slatest.slate.com/posts/2012/06/18/google_censorship_u_s_agencies_request_sharply_more_deletions_from_google.html.

State Department/USAID Efforts

The State Department has included Internet freedom as part of its global human rights agenda for several years. According to the State Department, it is U.S. policy to promote "a single Internet where all of humanity has equal access to knowledge and ideas. [The State Department's] work on Internet freedom is grounded in international commitments to free expression and the free flow of information as fundamental human rights."[46] In January 2010, Secretary of State Hillary Clinton delivered a major policy speech on Internet freedom, in which she raised concerns about "threats to the free flow of information" in China and other countries.[47] On February 15, 2011, Secretary Clinton reconfirmed the U.S. commitment to "protect and defend a free and open Internet," making particular reference to Egypt and Iran.[48] At the same time, the State Department continues to have concerns about increasing security and protecting intellectual and other property rights online, policies that some consider antithetical to the principle of Internet freedom. Some have asserted that U.S. willingness to condone friendly countries' use of digital surveillance technologies has bolstered claims by the governments of China and Russia, for example, that argue for tighter government controls over the Internet based on security grounds.

NetFreedom Taskforce

Since it was created in 2006 as the "Global Internet Freedom Taskforce" (GIFT), the NetFreedom Taskforce has coordinated State Department policy and outreach concerning Internet freedom.[49] The Taskforce is co-chaired by the Under Secretary of State for Democracy and Global Affairs and the Under Secretary of State for Economic, Energy, and Agricultural Affairs, and is implemented by the Bureau of Democracy, Human Rights, and Labor (DRL) and the Bureau of Economic, Energy, and Business Affairs (EEB), with participation by the State Department's regional bureaus and Office of the Legal Adviser. DRL, according to the State Department, leads human rights and democratization efforts related to Internet freedom, while EEB directs Internet freedom promotion activities as they relate to international corporate communications, business advocacy, and corporate responsibility issues.

The Taskforce coordinates State Department efforts to (1) monitor Internet freedom in foreign countries and report on findings in the annual State Department *Country Reports on Human Rights Practices*; (2) increase Internet access in countries where it is actively restricted or otherwise limited; and (3) respond to limits on or threats to Internet freedom through bilateral diplomacy and multilateral international fora.

---

[46] Department of State, "Internet Freedom," http://www.state.gov/e/eeb/cip/netfreedom/index htm.

[47] Hillary Rodham Clinton, "Remarks on Internet Freedom," January 21, 2010, http://www.state.gov/secretary/rm/2010/01/135519 htm.

[48] Hillary Rodham Clinton, "Internet Rights and Wrongs: Choices & Challenges in a Networked World," February 15, 2011, http://www.state.gov/secretary/rm/2011/02/156619 htm.

[49] In February 2011, the State Department announced the creation of the Office of the Coordinator for Cyber Issues in the Office of the Secretary. This Office was involved in the development of the President's International Strategy for Cyberspace, discussed above.

Internet Freedom Promotion Activities

During the early 2000s, U.S. Internet freedom efforts focused largely on censorship circumvention, particularly in China and Iran, with an important but limited impact. Focusing Internet freedom efforts on priority countries such as China and Iran has led some to question whether the United States considers Internet freedom a global principle or merely a selective tool of U.S. foreign policy.[50] Some experts began to advocate a broader approach, and State Department Internet freedom activities have in fact become more diverse. Programs now include a range of activities: censorship circumvention technology, privacy protection and online security (including secure e-mail and text communications), educating civil society groups in effective uses of the Internet, and developing ICT-based organizational and advocacy skills. It has been argued that this rapid expansion of funding for Internet freedom activities may endanger digital activism in some cases, as foreign support might delegitimize such movements in the eyes of local populations; provide targets and justification for persecution by repressive regimes; divert NGO attention from grass roots activism in favor of U.S.-government funded policy research and analysis; or co-opt digital activism in repressive countries for U.S. foreign policy purposes.[51]

Since 2008, Congress has appropriated approximately $95 million for State Department and USAID global Internet freedom efforts. The Secretary of State has requested $27.5 million for State Department and USAID Internet freedom activities for FY2013. Internet freedom funding is administered by DRL, State's Bureau of Near Eastern Affairs (NEA), and DCHA, and is allocated from the global Economic Support Fund (ESF), Human Rights and Democracy Fund (HRDF), and Near East Regional Democracy (NERD) program accounts.

State Department and USAID conduct several types of Internet freedom programs and activities. Technical assistance (circumvention and secure communications technology) focuses on approximately one dozen highly restrictive countries, particularly China and Iran. Advocacy assistance, which currently is less applicable to China due to its restrictive political environment, is provided to a broader set of countries. U.S. global program activities and objectives include the following:

1. Providing new Internet technologies that allow individuals in repressive environments to access online information and communicate freely on the Internet, including:

    - circumvention technologies that allow users to access blocked sites and censored information by using proxy servers and websites to get around firewalls;

    - Internet applications that allow users to access blocked and censored information while maintaining anonymity from government and other monitoring;

    - software that protects sites from cyberattack by repressive governments or other individuals seeking to censor or block information, and tools to enable attacked sites to protect information and quickly restore website operations after an attack;

---

[50] Sami ben Gharbia, *The Internet Freedom Fallacy and Arab Digital Activism*, FutureChallenges, Bertelsmann Stiftung, June 20, 2011, http://futurechallenges.org/local/the-internet-freedom-fallacy-and-the-arab-digital-activism/.

[51] Ibid.

- new technologies seeking to optimize Internet freedom on mobile communications technologies; and

- computer and communications hardware for activists to operate mobile Internet networks when repressive governments shut down Internet access.

2. Training human rights activists, civil society, and non-governmental organizations (NGOs) operating in repressive environments to effectively use Internet communications and circumvention technology, and avoid government monitoring and cyberattack;

3. Providing training in media assistance to support civil society groups and NGOs in the use of new media technologies to improve their online communication;

4. Responding to repression of Internet access, information, and speech by pressing repressive governments in both human rights and economic terms on the importance of Internet freedom, both privately and publicly;

5. Shaping international Internet freedom norms by leading international policy and standards discussions in multilateral fora, including the United Nations;

6. Monitoring Internet freedom conditions globally both in human rights reports and through Internet usage mapping software that can provide insight into trends in online information flows and relationships between populations online; and

7. Engaging the private sector to improve its efforts and expand its role in promoting Internet freedom globally (see discussion of the Global Network Initiative).

Broadcasting Board of Governors

A number of other U.S. government agencies also engage in Internet freedom promotion. The Broadcasting Board of Governors (BBG), which oversees U.S. international broadcasters including Voice of America (VOA) and Radio Free Asia (RFA), has been at the forefront of using counter-censorship or circumvention software for international Internet programming. During the 2000s, the BBG spent approximately $2 million annually to help enable Internet users in China and other Internet-restricting countries to access its websites via proxy servers. In recent years, funding has increased. For FY2011, Congress transferred $10 million in democracy promotion funding from the annual Bilateral Economic Assistance appropriation to the BBG for Internet censorship circumvention efforts,[52] and the agency received $9.1 million for FY2012. The BBG requested $11.6 million for these efforts in FY2013.

VOA reportedly sends e-mails to 8 million Chinese citizens daily with international and domestic news stories as well as information about how to use proxy servers in order to circumvent government censorship and thereby access VOA and other blocked websites. RFA implemented the Freedom2Connect program in recent years to research, develop, and deliver online tools for Internet users in China to securely browse online and send secure e-mail and other messages. RFA's program, "How to Scale the Chinese Firewall," is one of the broadcaster's efforts to inform the Chinese public on government censorship circumvention techniques. Some activists have

---

[52] Sec. 2121(g) of the Full-Year Continuing Appropriations Act, 2011 (Division B of P.L. 112-10).

called for greater funding for servers and enhanced bandwidth in order to keep up with China's Internet censorship system.

Congressional Activities[53]

Members of Congress have raised concerns, formed caucuses, funded programs, held hearings, and sponsored legislation regarding Internet freedom and related issues, with a focus on China. Congress appropriated $50 million for global Internet freedom efforts between FY2008-FY2010, $20 million in FY2011, and $25 million in FY2012. Program areas include censorship circumvention technology, Internet and mobile communications security training, media and advocacy skills, and public policy. The primary target countries of such efforts, particularly circumvention and secure communications programs, have been China and Iran. U.S. congressional committees and commissions have held hearings on the Internet and China, including the roles of U.S. Internet companies in China's censorship regime, cybersecurity, free trade in Internet services, and intellectual property rights (see below). The Department of State and the Congressional-Executive Commission on China include Internet freedom issues in their annual reports on human rights conditions in the PRC.[54]

Hearings

- U.S. Congress, House Committee on International Relations, Subcommittee on Africa, Global Human Rights and International Operations and Subcommittee on Asia and the Pacific, *The Internet in China: A Tool for Freedom or Suppression?*, February 15, 2006.

- House Committee on Foreign Affairs, *Yahoo! Inc.'s Provision of False Information to Congress*, November 6, 2007.

- U.S. Congress, Senate Committee on the Judiciary, Subcommittee on Human Rights and the Law, *Global Internet Freedom: Corporate Responsibility and the Rule of Law*, May 20, 2008.

- The Tom Lantos Human Rights Commission, *The State of Global Internet Freedom*, June 18, 2009.

- Congressional-Executive Commission on China, *China, the Internet, and Google*, March 1, 2010.

- Senate Committee on the Judiciary, Subcommittee on Human Rights and the Law, *Global Internet Freedom: Corporate Responsibility and the Rule of Law, Part II*, March 2, 2010.

- House Committee on Foreign Affairs, *The Google Predicament: Transforming U.S. Cyberspace Policy to Advance Democracy, Security, and Trade*, March 10, 2010.

---

[53] Written by Thomas Lum, Specialist in Asian Affairs.

[54] U.S. Department of State, *Country Reports on Human Rights Practices for 2011*, May 2012; China Congressional-Executive Commission on China, *Annual Report 2011*, October 10, 2011.

- Congressional-Executive Commission on China, *China's Censorship of the Internet and Social Media: The Human Toll and Trade Impact*, November 17, 2011.

- House Committee on Foreign Affairs, Subcommittee on Africa, Global Health, and Human Rights, *Promoting Global Internet Freedom*, December 8, 2011.

The Global Online Freedom Act

First introduced in 2006 as H.R. 4780, the Global Online Freedom Act (GOFA) has evolved through four congresses and reportedly has faced resistance from both the Administration and industry.[55] Since its introduction, various versions of the bill have sought the following: to establish an Office of Global Internet Freedom (OGIF); to require the Administration to submit an annual report on "Internet-restricting countries" and U.S. efforts to counter such interference; and to prevent U.S. companies from cooperating with governments that engage in censorship and other human rights abuses. Key provisions have included prohibiting U.S. companies from the following: storing personally identifiable information in Internet-restricting countries; providing such information to officials of such countries; and jamming U.S.-supported websites or content, subject to civil and criminal penalties (or to waivers in some cases). Under some versions of the bill, a U.S. business that provided a search engine or content hosting service in an Internet-restricting country would be required to disclose to the OGIF all information or data related to the censorship of information in response to the policies of that country.

The most recent version of the bill (H.R. 3605, introduced on December 8, 2011)[56] emphasizes due diligence and transparency while removing provisions that would establish the OGIF, prohibit companies from locating personally identifiable information in Internet-restricting countries or providing such information to local officials, and civil and criminal penalties. H.R. 3605 provides that U.S. companies located in Internet-restricting countries shall include in their annual reports "policies that address 'human rights due diligence' which reflect the Guidelines for Multinational Enterprises issued by the Organization for Economic Co-operation and Development" and policies pertaining to the collection of personally identifiable information. U.S. Internet service providers that filter or censor information are required to "provide users and customers with clear, prominent, and timely notice when access to specific content has been removed or blocked at the request of an Internet-restricting country." Other changes include the following: a new requirement that the United States Trade Representative submit a report on any trade-related issues that arise due to a foreign government's censorship policies; and a section on export controls of telecommunications equipment "that would serve the primary purpose of assisting, or be specifically configured to assist, a foreign government in acquiring the capability to carry out censorship, surveillance, or any other similar or related activity."

Some experts warned against earlier aspects of GOFA, for example, those provisions authorizing the U.S. Attorney General to determine when to bar U.S. Internet service providers from

---

[55] A similar, earlier bill, the Global Internet Freedom Act (H.R. 48), was introduced by Representative Chris Cox in 2003.

[56] H.R. 3605 was referred to the House Committee on Foreign Affairs, the House Ways and Means Committee, and the House Financial Services Committee. On January 1, 2012, the House Financial Services Committee referred the measure to the Subcommittee on Capital Markets and Government Sponsored Enterprises. On March 27, 2012, the House Foreign Affairs Committee, Subcommittee on Africa, Global Health and Human Rights, amended and approved the bill.

complying with foreign governments' requests for user information, and requiring U.S. companies to locate user data outside of Internet-restricting countries. Critics have suggested that the former provision would provide the Attorney General—and by extension the U.S. government—access to individual account information, which raises privacy concerns. The latter provision, they have argued, would do little to actually enhance use privacy, although it could reduce the reliability of services offered.[57]

Other analysts have expressed concern that current OGIF provisions requiring U.S. companies to disclose to the Securities and Exchange Commission any blocking or surveillance technology that they provide to Internet-restricting countries, and possibly prohibiting the sale of such items, may adversely affect political activists who may rely on such technology in such countries. Some policy experts have questioned the policy of designating some countries as "Internet restricting," which may place focus on some countries while ignoring other violators, overlook change in some countries, and result in the interference of diplomatic issues in Internet freedom efforts.[58]

Further Policy Considerations

As China enters a leadership transition in 2012-2013, Congress may consider how to uphold Internet freedom and regulate U.S. companies in an environment of growing tensions between state and society—of both greater freedom and heightened repression. General policy areas include funding, programming, and coordination. Congress may make decisions regarding how much money to provide to the State Department for global Internet freedom efforts, how to apportion appropriations for different types of program and target countries, and how to determine benchmarks for future support. Congress may attempt to find common ground between the Global Online Freedom Act and the Global Network Initiative, both of which attempt to promote human rights standards for ICT companies related to free expression and user privacy, company due diligence, and transparency. Congress may also consider ways to foster linkages between U.S. government, private sector, and international online freedom efforts.

---

[57] Rebecca MacKinnon, "Global Internet Freedom and the U.S. Government," op. cit.

[58] Emily Cadei, "Internet Freedom Bill Slowed by Resistance from Industry, Administration," *CQ Today*, March 26, 2012; Rebecca MacKinnon, "Global Internet Freedom and the U.S. Government," op. cit.

Appendix. Global Network Initiative: Membership, Core Documents and Implementation Process[59]

GNI Membership

The GNI is composed of:

- *Corporations*: Google, Yahoo!, and Microsoft. Facebook was granted "observer status" on May 3, 2012. Observer status is an opportunity for companies who are actively considering joining GNI to examine the initiative's programs as well as its principles on free expression and privacy. Observer status lasts for one non-renewable twelve-month term. Five seats remain open for future member companies.

- *Civil society organizations*: Human Rights Watch, Center for Democracy and Technology, Committee to Protect Journalists, and Human Rights First.[60]

- *Investors*: Calvert Group and Domini Social Investments.

- *Academics and academic organizations*: Colin Maclay (Berkman Center for Internet and Society, Harvard University) and Rebecca MacKinnon, New America Foundation (personal capacity).

Governments are not members of the GNI, but they are encouraged to support the goals of the GNI.

GNI Core Documents

There are three core documents that describe the Initiative's objectives and the key commitments of the participants:

- Principles on Freedom of Expression and Privacy

- Implementation Guidelines

- Governance, Accountability & Learning Framework

Principles on Freedom of Expression and Privacy

The Principles state the members' overarching commitment to collaborate in the advancement of user rights to freedom of expression and privacy. The Principles provide high-level guidance to the ICT industry on how to respect, protect, and advance user rights to freedom of expression and

---

[59] Written by Patricia Maloney Figliola, Specialist in Internet and Telecommunications Policy.

[60] Organizations not participating in the initiative who where involved in its development include Amnesty International and Reporters Without Borders.

privacy, including when faced with government demands for censorship and disclosure of users' personal information. Participating companies are committed to conducting "human rights risk assessments" that guide policy decisions. The Principles are intended to be applied globally and are based on internationally recognized laws and standards for human rights.[61]

Implementation Guidelines

The Implementation Guidelines provide more detailed guidance to ICT companies on how to put the Principles into practice, and also provide the framework for collaboration among companies, NGOs, investors and academics. When faced with demands to remove or limit access to content or restrict communications, participating companies are to:

- operate in a transparent manner when required to remove content or restrict access;

- disclose to users the applicable laws and policies requiring such action and the company's policies for responding to such demands; and

- provide timely notice to users when access to content has been blocked or communications limited due to government restrictions.

With respect to privacy, participating companies commit to assess the human rights risks associated with the collection, storage, and retention of personal information and to develop mitigation strategies.

The guidelines are regularly reviewed and revised to take into account actual experience, evolving circumstances, and stakeholder feedback.

Governance, Accountability & Learning Framework

The Governance, Accountability & Learning Framework sets out a multi-stakeholder governance structure, goals for collaboration, and a system of ensuring company. A system of independent third-party assessment of company compliance with the Principles and Implementation Guidelines is being phased in over three stages:

- In Phase One (which ended in December 2010) each participating company was to establish internal policies and procedures to implement the Principles, and the Board was to approve independence and competence criteria for the selection of independent assessors.

- In Phase Two (2011) independent assessors were to conduct process assessments of each participating company to review and evaluate their internal systems for implementing the Principles.

- In Phase Three (January 2012 onwards) the Board is to begin accrediting independent assessors to review the internal systems of companies and company responses to specific government demands implicating freedom of expression or

---

[61] The GNI's Principles are based on laws and standards such as the Universal Declaration of Human Rights (UDHR), the International Covenant on Civil and Political Rights (ICCPR), and the International Covenant on Economic, Social, and Cultural Rights.

privacy. Each participating company is to submit an annual report to the Organization. The assessors are to prepare reports explaining each company's responses to government demands and evaluating the effectiveness of the company's responses. Each company is to be given the opportunity to respond to the assessor's draft and final report. The Board of the Organization is to assess whether the company is in compliance with the Principles and its determination is to be made public. The Board of the Organization is to publish an annual report assessing each participating company's compliance with the Principles.

Current Activities

The GNI's goals for 2012 include:

- increasing membership across all constituencies, with a focus on new members in developing countries and emerging markets;

- deepening its relationships with companies across the ICT sector;

- carrying out the first Phase III assessments of the founding companies to see how implementation of the Principles is working in practice.

The development of Phase III of the assessment process has been cited as a key priority in 2012. The GNI has also commissioned a study to inform the development of a public engagement process that would enable the initiative to seek feedback from a broad set of stakeholders in a transparent and structured manner.

The first GNI Multi-Stakeholder Learning Forum was held in June 2012 in Washington, DC, inviting participants from around the world. The forum included:

- public dialogue on GNI's Principles and shared learning from implementation;

- the launch of GNI's research report on balancing free expression, privacy, national security, and law enforcement; and

- confidential dialogue among GNI members relating to human rights issues in ICTs.

Author Contact Information

Thomas Lum, Coordinator
Acting Section Research Manager/Specialist in
Asian Affairs
tlum@crs.loc.gov, 7-7616

Patricia Moloney Figliola
Specialist in Internet and Telecommunications
Policy
pfigliola@crs.loc.gov, 7-2508

Matthew C. Weed
Analyst in Foreign Policy Legislation
mweed@crs.loc.gov, 7-4589